NATIONAL GEOGRAPHIC

PIONEER EDITION

By Beth Geiger

CONTENTS

2   Spiders: Weaving Wonders

8   A Class Act

10 Which Is It?

12 Concept Check

Jumping spider

Spiders

Weaving Wonders

You might not like spiders. Yet these hunters are helpful animals. Earth would not be the same without them.

By Beth Geiger

Would you like to live with thousands of spiders? Chuck Kristensen does. He thinks spiders are cool. Lots of spiders share his home. He makes money by selling spiders.

Shy as a Spider?

Is this man crazy? Spiders are scary, right? Not really.

It is true that spiders can hurt people. A bite can leave a painful bump. Yet most spiders are shy. They rarely bite people.

Body Basics

Spiders may bug you. But they are not insects. They are **arachnids** (uh RAK nidz). They are related to scorpions and ticks.

A spider has two main body parts. One is the head. The other is the **abdomen,** or back part of a spider. Hair covers the spider. It helps the spider feel things.

Spiders also have fangs. Fangs are useful at mealtime. **Venom** comes out of them. Venom is a kind of poison. It can kill some animals. Spiders use venom to kill their meals.

Silk Factories

Spiders also have parts that make silk. Silk is a thin thread. It is stronger than steel.

Spiders use silk to do lots of things. They tie up their meals. They also make draglines. These are like safety ropes. They keep a spider from falling.

Female spiders even wrap their eggs with silk. That keeps the babies safe.

Do you know of another way spiders use silk? You guessed it! They use silk to make webs.

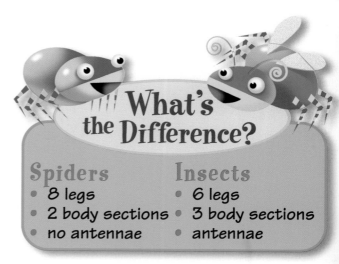

What's the Difference?

Spiders	Insects
• 8 legs	• 6 legs
• 2 body sections	• 3 body sections
• no antennae	• antennae

Mighty King.
The spider above is a king baboon spider. This hunter lives in Africa. It eats frogs, young birds, and other animals.

Web Wizard. The spider above is an orb weaver. It makes round webs. E.B. White's Charlotte was an orb weaver.

Caught in a Net. *The net above could be the last thing a cockroach or an ant sees. Net–casting spiders wait for animals to come close. When one does, the spider tosses the net to catch it.*

Color Change. *Some crab spiders (above) can turn yellow or white. Changing color can help a spider hide. Its color makes it look like part of a flower.*

Caught in a Web

Spiders use webs to catch meals. They weave their webs. Then they wait for a bug to come by.

Most bugs do not see webs. They fly right into them. They get stuck in the sticky silk. Then they become the spider's meal!

Wide World of Webs

Spiders make many kinds of webs. Some make orb webs. These webs look like wheels.

A purseweb spider lives inside a silk tube. The spider waits for a bug to walk by. Surprise! The spider bites it through the web. Then the spider eats it.

Sheetweb spiders weave flat webs. The webs stretch across bushes or grassy fields. They catch bugs near the ground.

Some spiders make webs like small nets. They toss their webs to catch dinner.

Hairy Legs. *This fuzzy beast (left) is a tarantula. Tarantulas hunt other creatures, including mice, frogs, birds, and snakes.*

Life Without a Web

Not all spiders make webs. How do others catch their dinner?

Trap-door spiders hide in holes. They make doors out of silk and dirt. At night, a spider opens the door to catch a meal.

Jumping spiders leap on their dinners. Other spiders go hunting.

Good and Hungry

We are lucky to have so many hungry spiders around. They eat a lot of pesky bugs.

Spiders might also help sick people. How? Their venom is used to make medicines. The medicines could help sick people.

You may never like spiders. But aren't you glad that spiders are in your world?

Wordwise

abdomen: back half of a spider's body

arachnid: spider or related animal

venom: poison

A Class Act

Look at the three animals below. Scientists think they are related. Why? These animals have a lot in common.

How are they alike? Study the pictures. What do you see?

This is how scientists sort living things into groups. They study them. They look for things that are the same.

Sorting It Out

Scientists group living things to show how they are related.

Scientists start by thinking big. They sort living things into five big groups. These are called kingdoms. Plants belong to one kingdom. Animals are in another.

Scientists also sort living things into many smaller groups.

Scorpion

Tick

Groups of Animals

People and spiders are animals. But we do not have much in common. So we share only one group—the kingdom.

Scorpions, spiders, and ticks have lots in common. So they share many groups. They are in the same kingdom, phylum, and class. They are called arachnids.

Striking Similarities

Arachnids may not seem like cousins. But they are all related!

How are they alike? They all have a hard body. They have two main body parts. They have eight legs. They all breathe air.

There are more than 60,000 kinds of arachnids. Most of them are spiders!

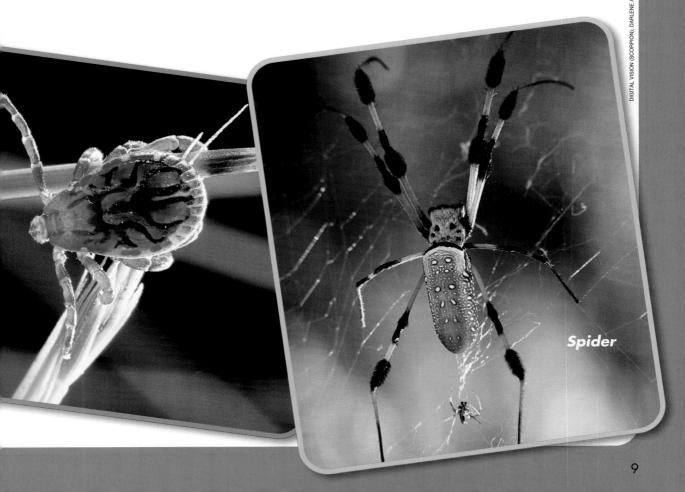

Spider

Which Is It?

How do you know whether an animal is a spider or an insect? Do what scientists do. Study its body. Look at these animals. Then answer the questions.

1 How many legs does each animal have? Hint: Some things that look like legs might not be.

2 How many body sections does each animal have? What does this tell you about the animal?

3 Which animals are arachnids? Which ones are insects? How did you decide which is which?

Spiders

Take a spin at answering these questions about spiders.

1 How does silk help a spider?

2 How do spiders use venom?

3 How do spiders catch meals?

4 How can you tell if an animal is a spider or an insect?

5 How do spiders help people?

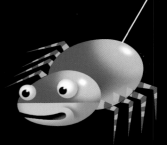